WINE TASTER'S JOURNAL

Wine Taster's Journal

DRINK, RATE, RECORD, AND REMEMBER

JOE ROBERTS

ROCKRIDGE PRESS

Interior and Cover Designer: John Clifford
Art Producer: Sue Bischofberger
Editor: Pam Kingsley
Production Editor: Matthew Burnett

Illustration © Claire Rollet, p. i.

Photography © ThinkDeep/iStock, cover; MarkSwallow/iStock, pp. ii and 136-137; EAQ/iStock, p. vi; Silberkorn/iStock, p. viii-1; Martí Sans/Stocksy, p. 8-9; supermimicry/iStock, p. 122-123; and aluxum/iStock, p. 130-131.

ISBN: Print 978-1-64739-044-0

R0

CONTENTS

INTRODUCTION

The best way to get a handle on what you like (or don't) in your wine is to journal your wine experiences. Journaling provides you with a record of your tastings, where you can decipher your own personal wine "code," revealing what aspects make up the wines that you most love to drink—or most want to avoid entirely from now on.

This journal is designed to help you do exactly that. It collects some of the most frequently used wine descriptors for aromas and flavors, so you won't have to struggle with figuring out exactly how to describe what you're tasting. It includes multiple-choice-style options for quickly recording how a particular wine feels in your mouth. And it has spots for you to record every piece of relevant information that you can think of for the wine that you're drinking.

You're in charge here, and the journal is a tool to help you record your wine impressions as efficiently and thoroughly as possible. There are no right or wrong answers. What matters is that the results of the journaling make sense to *you*, so that the future stops on your wine journey are as pleasurable as possible.

TASTING
101

The Basics of Wine Tasting

Tasting mindfully isn't the sole purview of wine experts. It's a skill that anyone can develop and hone—it just takes practice. Fortunately, the homework is pretty awesome.

Here are the most important aspects to keep in mind when tasting a wine to evaluate and journal it effectively. Each step has a practical purpose, and none of them requires any drama or fanfare. For each step, take a few moments to focus and really examine what you're experiencing. That will make the journaling (and the learning) more valuable, more detailed, and a lot more fun.

APPEARANCE

In examining a wine's appearance, you're not only performing a quick check on its overall health, but also enjoying its wonderful palette of colors before sampling its flavors on your palate. Obviously, this step will tell you if the wine is red, white, rosé, or sparkling.

If possible, tilt the glass of wine slightly and hold it against a white background to see what color shades the wine has at its center and its rim, and how opaque or clear it is. For sparkling wine, the size of the bubbles can provide a clue as to the wine's quality and mouthfeel (smaller bubbles are usually better and feel more elegant in the mouth).

Younger reds will have more color, all the way out to the rim, while younger whites will have less. As they age, red wines lose color and show "brick" red (tinged a bit with orange) at the edges, while whites take on deeper, honeyed hues. Cloudiness in the wine could be a sign of faults; if something looks amiss, it probably is. Most red wine sediment is harmless but has a texture like coffee grounds and should be avoided if possible (if you see sediment in your glass, it's time for a more careful pour).

SMELL

This is the most important step and the one in which most of a wine's complexity (and taste) is perceived in what we call the wine's "nose," a shorthand term for describing how a wine smells in the glass. Swirling the wine in the glass for a moment or two will help release its volatile aroma compounds, making them easier to detect and journal. Not all wine aromas are good ones, and if a wine smells off (e.g., skunky or musty), then there is almost certainly something wrong with it. When you're ready, take a few sniffs from the edge of the glass and note what aromas you're picking up from the wine. Some wines will have clear, intense aromas, while others will require more attention and thought (and time) to reveal themselves.

For some wines, you may have to come back to the glass after several minutes and take even more sniffs to note how the wine is evolving after being exposed to the air and warming up in the glass. The more you notice, the more you should record in your journal, emphasizing which aromas you like most (and least).

TASTE

Tasting is where you get a sense of a wine's texture, direct flavors, and the indirect aromas that are released after it hits your tongue. Following are the things that you want to look for after taking a sip and swishing the wine around in your mouth for a few moments.

ACIDITY impacts how "energetic" a wine feels in your mouth (meaning its sense of vivacity and prickliness). Acidity also helps to balance out any sweetness in the wine. Think of acidity like adding a spritz of lemon to a drink or a meal: too much and it feels bracing and acerbic; too little and it will feel flat or flabby.

TANNINS come from grape skins, grape seeds and stems, and barrel aging; they are most commonly found in red wines. They help give the wine stability and a sense of structure in the mouth. Think of them like the amount of time that you steep black tea: too much and the wine will feel grating and astringent across your mouth and gums; too little and it will feel out of balance or overly fruity. Different grapes naturally have fewer tannins (like Pinot Noir) or more tannins (like Cabernet Sauvignon).

BODY affects a wine's "weight" on your palate. Fuller, richer, riper wines with higher alcohol content will feel rounder and more powerful in the mouth, giving the wine a sense of heaviness. If overly powerful, a wine can feel "hot" in the mouth from its alcohol. Lighter wines with less alcohol will feel lighter, livelier, more focused, and refreshing. If the alcohol volume is too low compared with a wine's other qualities, it can feel too "thin" and weak in the mouth.

TEXTURE is a wine's overall physical impression in your mouth. Do its various elements feel balanced and harmonious? Light and airy? Smooth like silk? Or prickly or rough? Along with body, texture is a major factor when pairing wine with food, and different people will prefer different textures just as they prefer different aromas and flavors. There's no "right" answer when it comes to texture, but more balanced textures are generally considered higher quality than those that are dominated by one or two aspects.

FINISH

After swallowing (or spitting out) a taste of wine, note what happens afterward. Usually, you will detect aromas and flavors that linger for varying amounts of time. This is the wine's "finish," and higher quality wines can have one that lasts for a minute or even longer. What's on the finish is just as important as how long it lasts. Is it pleasant? Are the flavors and aromas consistent with those on the nose and on the palate? Like a great meal, the more harmonious the combination of elements is, the higher the quality of the total experience.

It's easy for tasters to skip this step; don't be one of those tasters. The finish is often the difference-maker that separates wines that are pretty good from wines that are exceptional.

TASTING
NOTES

WINE:

PRODUCER:

| VINTAGE: | ALCOHOL %: | PRICE: |

REGION/COUNTRY:

GRAPE(S):

PLACE AND DATE PURCHASED:

| DATE TASTED: | IMPORTER/DISTRIBUTOR: |

COLOR/STYLE: ❑ Red ❑ White ❑ Rosé
❑ Sparkling ❑ Dessert ❑ Other

COLOR:

AROMAS:

DRY/SWEET: ❑ Bone-dry ❑ Dry ❑ Off-dry
❑ Medium-sweet ❑ Sweet

TANNINS: ❑ Low (easy to drink)   ❑ Medium (balanced)
❑ High (bitter)

ACIDITY: ❑ Flat (very low)   ❑ Soft (low)
❑ Balanced   ❑ High (lively)   ❑ Very high (bracing)

BODY: ❑ Light   ❑ Medium   ❑ Full

TEXTURE: ❑ Smooth   ❑ Light   ❑ Prickly/acidic
❑ Balanced   ❑ Rough

TASTE:

_____

FINISH: ❑ Short   ❑ Medium   ❑ Long

FOOD PAIRED WITH IT:

_____

PAIRING SUCCESS: ❑ Disaster   ❑ Okay, but not great
❑ Pretty good   ❑ Fantastic

ADDITIONAL COMMENTS:

_____

_____

_____

YOUR RATING:
☆   ☆☆   ☆☆☆   ☆☆☆☆   ☆☆☆☆☆

WINE:

_____

PRODUCER:

_____

VINTAGE: | ALCOHOL %: | PRICE:

_____

REGION/COUNTRY:

_____

GRAPE(S):

_____

PLACE AND DATE PURCHASED:

_____

DATE TASTED: | IMPORTER/DISTRIBUTOR:

_____

COLOR/STYLE: ❑ Red ❑ White ❑ Rosé
❑ Sparkling ❑ Dessert ❑ Other

COLOR:

_____

AROMAS:

_____

DRY/SWEET: ❑ Bone-dry ❑ Dry ❑ Off-dry
❑ Medium-sweet ❑ Sweet

TANNINS: ❑ Low (easy to drink)   ❑ Medium (balanced)
❑ High (bitter)

ACIDITY: ❑ Flat (very low)   ❑ Soft (low)
❑ Balanced   ❑ High (lively)   ❑ Very high (bracing)

BODY: ❑ Light   ❑ Medium   ❑ Full

TEXTURE: ❑ Smooth   ❑ Light   ❑ Prickly/acidic
❑ Balanced   ❑ Rough

TASTE:

FINISH: ❑ Short   ❑ Medium   ❑ Long

FOOD PAIRED WITH IT:

PAIRING SUCCESS: ❑ Disaster   ❑ Okay, but not great
❑ Pretty good   ❑ Fantastic

ADDITIONAL COMMENTS:

YOUR RATING:
☆   ☆☆   ☆☆☆   ☆☆☆☆   ☆☆☆☆☆

WINE:

PRODUCER:

| VINTAGE: | ALCOHOL %: | PRICE: |

REGION/COUNTRY:

GRAPE(S):

PLACE AND DATE PURCHASED:

| DATE TASTED: | IMPORTER/DISTRIBUTOR: |

COLOR/STYLE: ❑ Red   ❑ White   ❑ Rosé
❑ Sparkling   ❑ Dessert   ❑ Other

COLOR:

AROMAS:

DRY/SWEET: ❑ Bone-dry   ❑ Dry   ❑ Off-dry
❑ Medium-sweet   ❑ Sweet

TANNINS: ❑ Low (easy to drink) ❑ Medium (balanced)
❑ High (bitter)

ACIDITY: ❑ Flat (very low) ❑ Soft (low)
❑ Balanced ❑ High (lively) ❑ Very high (bracing)

BODY: ❑ Light ❑ Medium ❑ Full

TEXTURE: ❑ Smooth ❑ Light ❑ Prickly/acidic
❑ Balanced ❑ Rough

TASTE:

_____

FINISH: ❑ Short ❑ Medium ❑ Long

FOOD PAIRED WITH IT:

_____

PAIRING SUCCESS: ❑ Disaster ❑ Okay, but not great
❑ Pretty good ❑ Fantastic

ADDITIONAL COMMENTS:

_____

_____

_____

YOUR RATING:
☆   ☆☆   ☆☆☆   ☆☆☆☆   ☆☆☆☆☆

WINE:

_____

PRODUCER:

_____

| VINTAGE: | ALCOHOL %: | PRICE: |

_____

REGION/COUNTRY:

_____

GRAPE(S):

_____

PLACE AND DATE PURCHASED:

_____

| DATE TASTED: | IMPORTER/DISTRIBUTOR: |

_____

COLOR/STYLE: ❑ Red   ❑ White   ❑ Rosé
❑ Sparkling   ❑ Dessert   ❑ Other

COLOR:

_____

AROMAS:

_____

DRY/SWEET: ❑ Bone-dry   ❑ Dry   ❑ Off-dry
❑ Medium-sweet   ❑ Sweet

TANNINS: ❑ Low (easy to drink)   ❑ Medium (balanced)
❑ High (bitter)

ACIDITY: ❑ Flat (very low)   ❑ Soft (low)
❑ Balanced   ❑ High (lively)   ❑ Very high (bracing)

BODY: ❑ Light   ❑ Medium   ❑ Full

TEXTURE: ❑ Smooth   ❑ Light   ❑ Prickly/acidic
❑ Balanced   ❑ Rough

TASTE:

_____

FINISH: ❑ Short   ❑ Medium   ❑ Long

FOOD PAIRED WITH IT:

_____

PAIRING SUCCESS: ❑ Disaster   ❑ Okay, but not great
❑ Pretty good   ❑ Fantastic

ADDITIONAL COMMENTS:

_____

_____

_____

YOUR RATING:
☆   ☆☆   ☆☆☆   ☆☆☆☆   ☆☆☆☆☆

WINE:

_____

PRODUCER:

_____

| VINTAGE: | ALCOHOL %: | PRICE: |

_____

REGION/COUNTRY:

_____

GRAPE(S):

_____

PLACE AND DATE PURCHASED:

_____

| DATE TASTED: | IMPORTER/DISTRIBUTOR: |

_____

COLOR/STYLE: ❏ Red ❏ White ❏ Rosé
❏ Sparkling ❏ Dessert ❏ Other

COLOR:

_____

AROMAS:

_____

DRY/SWEET: ❏ Bone-dry ❏ Dry ❏ Off-dry
❏ Medium-sweet ❏ Sweet

TANNINS: ❑ Low (easy to drink) ❑ Medium (balanced)
❑ High (bitter)

ACIDITY: ❑ Flat (very low) ❑ Soft (low)
❑ Balanced ❑ High (lively) ❑ Very high (bracing)

BODY: ❑ Light ❑ Medium ❑ Full

TEXTURE: ❑ Smooth ❑ Light ❑ Prickly/acidic
❑ Balanced ❑ Rough

TASTE:

_____

FINISH: ❑ Short ❑ Medium ❑ Long

FOOD PAIRED WITH IT:

_____

PAIRING SUCCESS: ❑ Disaster ❑ Okay, but not great
❑ Pretty good ❑ Fantastic

ADDITIONAL COMMENTS:

_____

_____

_____

YOUR RATING:
☆ ☆☆ ☆☆☆ ☆☆☆☆ ☆☆☆☆☆

WINE:

_____

PRODUCER:

_____

| VINTAGE: | ALCOHOL %: | PRICE: |

_____

REGION/COUNTRY:

_____

GRAPE(S):

_____

PLACE AND DATE PURCHASED:

_____

| DATE TASTED: | IMPORTER/DISTRIBUTOR: |

_____

COLOR/STYLE: ❑ Red   ❑ White   ❑ Rosé
❑ Sparkling   ❑ Dessert   ❑ Other

COLOR:

_____

AROMAS:

_____

DRY/SWEET: ❑ Bone-dry   ❑ Dry   ❑ Off-dry
❑ Medium-sweet   ❑ Sweet

TANNINS: ❏ Low (easy to drink)   ❏ Medium (balanced)
❏ High (bitter)

ACIDITY: ❏ Flat (very low)   ❏ Soft (low)
❏ Balanced   ❏ High (lively)   ❏ Very high (bracing)

BODY: ❏ Light   ❏ Medium   ❏ Full

TEXTURE: ❏ Smooth   ❏ Light   ❏ Prickly/acidic
❏ Balanced   ❏ Rough

TASTE:

FINISH: ❏ Short   ❏ Medium   ❏ Long

FOOD PAIRED WITH IT:

PAIRING SUCCESS: ❏ Disaster   ❏ Okay, but not great
❏ Pretty good   ❏ Fantastic

ADDITIONAL COMMENTS:

YOUR RATING:
☆   ☆☆   ☆☆☆   ☆☆☆☆   ☆☆☆☆☆

WINE:

PRODUCER:

| **VINTAGE:** | **ALCOHOL %:** | **PRICE:** |

REGION/COUNTRY:

GRAPE(S):

PLACE AND DATE PURCHASED:

| **DATE TASTED:** | **IMPORTER/DISTRIBUTOR:** |

COLOR/STYLE: ❑ Red ❑ White ❑ Rosé
❑ Sparkling ❑ Dessert ❑ Other

COLOR:

AROMAS:

DRY/SWEET: ❑ Bone-dry ❑ Dry ❑ Off-dry
❑ Medium-sweet ❑ Sweet

TANNINS: ❑ Low (easy to drink) ❑ Medium (balanced)
❑ High (bitter)

ACIDITY: ❑ Flat (very low) ❑ Soft (low)
❑ Balanced ❑ High (lively) ❑ Very high (bracing)

BODY: ❑ Light ❑ Medium ❑ Full

TEXTURE: ❑ Smooth ❑ Light ❑ Prickly/acidic
❑ Balanced ❑ Rough

TASTE:

FINISH: ❑ Short ❑ Medium ❑ Long

FOOD PAIRED WITH IT:

PAIRING SUCCESS: ❑ Disaster ❑ Okay, but not great
❑ Pretty good ❑ Fantastic

ADDITIONAL COMMENTS:

YOUR RATING:
☆   ☆☆   ☆☆☆   ☆☆☆☆   ☆☆☆☆☆

WINE:

_____

PRODUCER:

_____

| VINTAGE: | ALCOHOL %: | PRICE: |

_____

REGION/COUNTRY:

_____

GRAPE(S):

_____

PLACE AND DATE PURCHASED:

_____

| DATE TASTED: | IMPORTER/DISTRIBUTOR: |

_____

COLOR/STYLE: ❑ Red   ❑ White   ❑ Rosé
❑ Sparkling   ❑ Dessert   ❑ Other

COLOR:

_____

AROMAS:

_____

DRY/SWEET: ❑ Bone-dry   ❑ Dry   ❑ Off-dry
❑ Medium-sweet   ❑ Sweet

TANNINS: ❑ Low (easy to drink) ❑ Medium (balanced)
❑ High (bitter)

ACIDITY: ❑ Flat (very low) ❑ Soft (low)
❑ Balanced ❑ High (lively) ❑ Very high (bracing)

BODY: ❑ Light ❑ Medium ❑ Full

TEXTURE: ❑ Smooth ❑ Light ❑ Prickly/acidic
❑ Balanced ❑ Rough

TASTE:

FINISH: ❑ Short ❑ Medium ❑ Long

FOOD PAIRED WITH IT:

PAIRING SUCCESS: ❑ Disaster ❑ Okay, but not great
❑ Pretty good ❑ Fantastic

ADDITIONAL COMMENTS:

YOUR RATING:
☆   ☆☆   ☆☆☆   ☆☆☆☆   ☆☆☆☆☆

WINE:

_____

PRODUCER:

_____

| **VINTAGE:** | **ALCOHOL %:** | **PRICE:** |

_____

REGION/COUNTRY:

_____

GRAPE(S):

_____

PLACE AND DATE PURCHASED:

_____

| **DATE TASTED:** | **IMPORTER/DISTRIBUTOR:** |

_____

COLOR/STYLE: ❑ Red   ❑ White   ❑ Rosé
❑ Sparkling   ❑ Dessert   ❑ Other

COLOR:

_____

AROMAS:

_____

DRY/SWEET: ❑ Bone-dry   ❑ Dry   ❑ Off-dry
❑ Medium-sweet   ❑ Sweet

TANNINS: ❑ Low (easy to drink)   ❑ Medium (balanced)
❑ High (bitter)

ACIDITY: ❑ Flat (very low)   ❑ Soft (low)
❑ Balanced   ❑ High (lively)   ❑ Very high (bracing)

BODY: ❑ Light   ❑ Medium   ❑ Full

TEXTURE: ❑ Smooth   ❑ Light   ❑ Prickly/acidic
❑ Balanced   ❑ Rough

TASTE:

_____

FINISH: ❑ Short   ❑ Medium   ❑ Long

FOOD PAIRED WITH IT:

_____

PAIRING SUCCESS: ❑ Disaster   ❑ Okay, but not great
❑ Pretty good   ❑ Fantastic

ADDITIONAL COMMENTS:

_____

_____

_____

YOUR RATING:
☆   ☆☆   ☆☆☆   ☆☆☆☆   ☆☆☆☆☆

WINE:

_____

PRODUCER:

_____

VINTAGE: | ALCOHOL %: | PRICE:

_____

REGION/COUNTRY:

_____

GRAPE(S):

_____

PLACE AND DATE PURCHASED:

_____

DATE TASTED: | IMPORTER/DISTRIBUTOR:

_____

COLOR/STYLE: ❑ Red ❑ White ❑ Rosé
❑ Sparkling ❑ Dessert ❑ Other

COLOR:

_____

AROMAS:

_____

DRY/SWEET: ❑ Bone-dry ❑ Dry ❑ Off-dry
❑ Medium-sweet ❑ Sweet

TANNINS: ❑ Low (easy to drink) ❑ Medium (balanced)
❑ High (bitter)

ACIDITY: ❑ Flat (very low) ❑ Soft (low)
❑ Balanced ❑ High (lively) ❑ Very high (bracing)

BODY: ❑ Light ❑ Medium ❑ Full

TEXTURE: ❑ Smooth ❑ Light ❑ Prickly/acidic
❑ Balanced ❑ Rough

TASTE:

_____

FINISH: ❑ Short ❑ Medium ❑ Long

FOOD PAIRED WITH IT:

_____

PAIRING SUCCESS: ❑ Disaster ❑ Okay, but not great
❑ Pretty good ❑ Fantastic

ADDITIONAL COMMENTS:

_____

_____

_____

YOUR RATING:
☆   ☆☆   ☆☆☆   ☆☆☆☆   ☆☆☆☆☆

WINE:

PRODUCER:

VINTAGE: | ALCOHOL %: | PRICE:

REGION/COUNTRY:

GRAPE(S):

PLACE AND DATE PURCHASED:

DATE TASTED: | IMPORTER/DISTRIBUTOR:

COLOR/STYLE: ❑ Red ❑ White ❑ Rosé
❑ Sparkling ❑ Dessert ❑ Other

COLOR:

AROMAS:

DRY/SWEET: ❑ Bone-dry ❑ Dry ❑ Off-dry
❑ Medium-sweet ❑ Sweet

TANNINS: ❑ Low (easy to drink)   ❑ Medium (balanced)
❑ High (bitter)

ACIDITY: ❑ Flat (very low)   ❑ Soft (low)
❑ Balanced   ❑ High (lively)   ❑ Very high (bracing)

BODY: ❑ Light   ❑ Medium   ❑ Full

TEXTURE: ❑ Smooth   ❑ Light   ❑ Prickly/acidic
❑ Balanced   ❑ Rough

TASTE:

FINISH: ❑ Short   ❑ Medium   ❑ Long

FOOD PAIRED WITH IT:

PAIRING SUCCESS: ❑ Disaster   ❑ Okay, but not great
❑ Pretty good   ❑ Fantastic

ADDITIONAL COMMENTS:

YOUR RATING:

☆   ☆☆   ☆☆☆   ☆☆☆☆   ☆☆☆☆☆

WINE:

_____

PRODUCER:

_____

VINTAGE:	ALCOHOL %:	PRICE:

REGION/COUNTRY:

_____

GRAPE(S):

_____

PLACE AND DATE PURCHASED:

_____

DATE TASTED:	IMPORTER/DISTRIBUTOR:

COLOR/STYLE: ❑ Red   ❑ White   ❑ Rosé
❑ Sparkling   ❑ Dessert   ❑ Other

COLOR:

_____

AROMAS:

_____

DRY/SWEET: ❑ Bone-dry   ❑ Dry   ❑ Off-dry
❑ Medium-sweet   ❑ Sweet

TANNINS: ❑ Low (easy to drink) ❑ Medium (balanced)
❑ High (bitter)

ACIDITY: ❑ Flat (very low) ❑ Soft (low)
❑ Balanced ❑ High (lively) ❑ Very high (bracing)

BODY: ❑ Light ❑ Medium ❑ Full

TEXTURE: ❑ Smooth ❑ Light ❑ Prickly/acidic
❑ Balanced ❑ Rough

TASTE:

_____

FINISH: ❑ Short ❑ Medium ❑ Long

FOOD PAIRED WITH IT:

_____

PAIRING SUCCESS: ❑ Disaster ❑ Okay, but not great
❑ Pretty good ❑ Fantastic

ADDITIONAL COMMENTS:

_____

_____

_____

YOUR RATING:
☆   ☆☆   ☆☆☆   ☆☆☆☆   ☆☆☆☆☆

WINE:

PRODUCER:

VINTAGE: | **ALCOHOL %:** | **PRICE:**

REGION/COUNTRY:

GRAPE(S):

PLACE AND DATE PURCHASED:

DATE TASTED: | **IMPORTER/DISTRIBUTOR:**

COLOR/STYLE: ❑ Red   ❑ White   ❑ Rosé
❑ Sparkling   ❑ Dessert   ❑ Other

COLOR:

AROMAS:

DRY/SWEET: ❑ Bone-dry   ❑ Dry   ❑ Off-dry
❑ Medium-sweet   ❑ Sweet

TANNINS: ❑ Low (easy to drink)   ❑ Medium (balanced)
❑ High (bitter)

ACIDITY: ❑ Flat (very low)   ❑ Soft (low)
❑ Balanced   ❑ High (lively)   ❑ Very high (bracing)

BODY: ❑ Light   ❑ Medium   ❑ Full

TEXTURE: ❑ Smooth   ❑ Light   ❑ Prickly/acidic
❑ Balanced   ❑ Rough

TASTE:

_____

FINISH: ❑ Short   ❑ Medium   ❑ Long

FOOD PAIRED WITH IT:

_____

PAIRING SUCCESS: ❑ Disaster   ❑ Okay, but not great
❑ Pretty good   ❑ Fantastic

ADDITIONAL COMMENTS:

_____

_____

_____

YOUR RATING:
☆   ☆☆   ☆☆☆   ☆☆☆☆   ☆☆☆☆☆

WINE:

PRODUCER:

| VINTAGE: | ALCOHOL %: | PRICE: |

REGION/COUNTRY:

GRAPE(S):

PLACE AND DATE PURCHASED:

| DATE TASTED: | IMPORTER/DISTRIBUTOR: |

COLOR/STYLE: ❑ Red ❑ White ❑ Rosé
❑ Sparkling ❑ Dessert ❑ Other

COLOR:

AROMAS:

DRY/SWEET: ❑ Bone-dry ❑ Dry ❑ Off-dry
❑ Medium-sweet ❑ Sweet

TANNINS: ❑ Low (easy to drink)   ❑ Medium (balanced)
❑ High (bitter)

ACIDITY: ❑ Flat (very low)   ❑ Soft (low)
❑ Balanced   ❑ High (lively)   ❑ Very high (bracing)

BODY: ❑ Light   ❑ Medium   ❑ Full

TEXTURE: ❑ Smooth   ❑ Light   ❑ Prickly/acidic
❑ Balanced   ❑ Rough

TASTE:

_____

FINISH: ❑ Short   ❑ Medium   ❑ Long

FOOD PAIRED WITH IT:

_____

PAIRING SUCCESS: ❑ Disaster   ❑ Okay, but not great
❑ Pretty good   ❑ Fantastic

ADDITIONAL COMMENTS:

_____

_____

_____

YOUR RATING:
☆   ☆☆   ☆☆☆   ☆☆☆☆   ☆☆☆☆☆

WINE:

PRODUCER:

| **VINTAGE:** | **ALCOHOL %:** | **PRICE:** |

REGION/COUNTRY:

GRAPE(S):

PLACE AND DATE PURCHASED:

| **DATE TASTED:** | **IMPORTER/DISTRIBUTOR:** |

COLOR/STYLE: ❏ Red ❏ White ❏ Rosé
❏ Sparkling ❏ Dessert ❏ Other

COLOR:

AROMAS:

DRY/SWEET: ❏ Bone-dry ❏ Dry ❏ Off-dry
❏ Medium-sweet ❏ Sweet

TANNINS: ❑ Low (easy to drink)   ❑ Medium (balanced)
❑ High (bitter)

ACIDITY: ❑ Flat (very low)   ❑ Soft (low)
❑ Balanced   ❑ High (lively)   ❑ Very high (bracing)

BODY: ❑ Light   ❑ Medium   ❑ Full

TEXTURE: ❑ Smooth   ❑ Light   ❑ Prickly/acidic
❑ Balanced   ❑ Rough

TASTE:

_____

FINISH: ❑ Short   ❑ Medium   ❑ Long

FOOD PAIRED WITH IT:

_____

PAIRING SUCCESS: ❑ Disaster   ❑ Okay, but not great
❑ Pretty good   ❑ Fantastic

ADDITIONAL COMMENTS:

_____

_____

_____

YOUR RATING:
☆   ☆☆   ☆☆☆   ☆☆☆☆   ☆☆☆☆☆

WINE:

PRODUCER:

VINTAGE: | ALCOHOL %: | PRICE:

REGION/COUNTRY:

GRAPE(S):

PLACE AND DATE PURCHASED:

DATE TASTED: | IMPORTER/DISTRIBUTOR:

COLOR/STYLE: ❑ Red ❑ White ❑ Rosé
❑ Sparkling ❑ Dessert ❑ Other

COLOR:

AROMAS:

DRY/SWEET: ❑ Bone-dry ❑ Dry ❑ Off-dry
❑ Medium-sweet ❑ Sweet

TANNINS: ❑ Low (easy to drink)   ❑ Medium (balanced)
❑ High (bitter)

ACIDITY: ❑ Flat (very low)   ❑ Soft (low)
❑ Balanced   ❑ High (lively)   ❑ Very high (bracing)

BODY: ❑ Light   ❑ Medium   ❑ Full

TEXTURE: ❑ Smooth   ❑ Light   ❑ Prickly/acidic
❑ Balanced   ❑ Rough

TASTE:

_____

FINISH: ❑ Short   ❑ Medium   ❑ Long

FOOD PAIRED WITH IT:

_____

PAIRING SUCCESS: ❑ Disaster   ❑ Okay, but not great
❑ Pretty good   ❑ Fantastic

ADDITIONAL COMMENTS:

_____

_____

_____

YOUR RATING:
☆   ☆☆   ☆☆☆   ☆☆☆☆   ☆☆☆☆☆

WINE:

_____

PRODUCER:

_____

| VINTAGE: | ALCOHOL %: | PRICE: |

_____

REGION/COUNTRY:

_____

GRAPE(S):

_____

PLACE AND DATE PURCHASED:

_____

| DATE TASTED: | IMPORTER/DISTRIBUTOR: |

_____

COLOR/STYLE: ❑ Red   ❑ White   ❑ Rosé
❑ Sparkling   ❑ Dessert   ❑ Other

COLOR:

_____

AROMAS:

_____

DRY/SWEET: ❑ Bone-dry   ❑ Dry   ❑ Off-dry
❑ Medium-sweet   ❑ Sweet

TANNINS: ❑ Low (easy to drink) ❑ Medium (balanced)
❑ High (bitter)

ACIDITY: ❑ Flat (very low) ❑ Soft (low)
❑ Balanced ❑ High (lively) ❑ Very high (bracing)

BODY: ❑ Light ❑ Medium ❑ Full

TEXTURE: ❑ Smooth ❑ Light ❑ Prickly/acidic
❑ Balanced ❑ Rough

TASTE:

_____

FINISH: ❑ Short ❑ Medium ❑ Long

FOOD PAIRED WITH IT:

_____

PAIRING SUCCESS: ❑ Disaster ❑ Okay, but not great
❑ Pretty good ❑ Fantastic

ADDITIONAL COMMENTS:

_____

_____

_____

YOUR RATING:
☆ ☆☆ ☆☆☆ ☆☆☆☆ ☆☆☆☆☆

WINE:

_____

PRODUCER:

_____

VINTAGE:	ALCOHOL %:	PRICE:

REGION/COUNTRY:

_____

GRAPE(S):

_____

PLACE AND DATE PURCHASED:

_____

DATE TASTED:	IMPORTER/DISTRIBUTOR:

COLOR/STYLE: ❑ Red ❑ White ❑ Rosé
❑ Sparkling ❑ Dessert ❑ Other

COLOR:

_____

AROMAS:

_____

DRY/SWEET: ❑ Bone-dry ❑ Dry ❑ Off-dry
❑ Medium-sweet ❑ Sweet

TANNINS: ❏ Low (easy to drink)   ❏ Medium (balanced)
❏ High (bitter)

ACIDITY: ❏ Flat (very low)   ❏ Soft (low)
❏ Balanced   ❏ High (lively)   ❏ Very high (bracing)

BODY: ❏ Light   ❏ Medium   ❏ Full

TEXTURE: ❏ Smooth   ❏ Light   ❏ Prickly/acidic
❏ Balanced   ❏ Rough

TASTE:

FINISH: ❏ Short   ❏ Medium   ❏ Long

FOOD PAIRED WITH IT:

PAIRING SUCCESS: ❏ Disaster   ❏ Okay, but not great
❏ Pretty good   ❏ Fantastic

ADDITIONAL COMMENTS:

YOUR RATING:
☆   ☆☆   ☆☆☆   ☆☆☆☆   ☆☆☆☆☆

WINE:

PRODUCER:

VINTAGE: | ALCOHOL %: | PRICE:

REGION/COUNTRY:

GRAPE(S):

PLACE AND DATE PURCHASED:

DATE TASTED: | IMPORTER/DISTRIBUTOR:

COLOR/STYLE: ❑ Red ❑ White ❑ Rosé
❑ Sparkling ❑ Dessert ❑ Other

COLOR:

AROMAS:

DRY/SWEET: ❑ Bone-dry ❑ Dry ❑ Off-dry
❑ Medium-sweet ❑ Sweet

TANNINS: ❑ Low (easy to drink)   ❑ Medium (balanced)
❑ High (bitter)

ACIDITY: ❑ Flat (very low)   ❑ Soft (low)
❑ Balanced   ❑ High (lively)   ❑ Very high (bracing)

BODY: ❑ Light   ❑ Medium   ❑ Full

TEXTURE: ❑ Smooth   ❑ Light   ❑ Prickly/acidic
❑ Balanced   ❑ Rough

TASTE:

FINISH: ❑ Short   ❑ Medium   ❑ Long

FOOD PAIRED WITH IT:

PAIRING SUCCESS: ❑ Disaster   ❑ Okay, but not great
❑ Pretty good   ❑ Fantastic

ADDITIONAL COMMENTS:

YOUR RATING:
☆   ☆☆   ☆☆☆   ☆☆☆☆   ☆☆☆☆☆

WINE:

PRODUCER:

| VINTAGE: | ALCOHOL %: | PRICE: |

REGION/COUNTRY:

GRAPE(S):

PLACE AND DATE PURCHASED:

| DATE TASTED: | IMPORTER/DISTRIBUTOR: |

COLOR/STYLE: ❏ Red ❏ White ❏ Rosé
❏ Sparkling ❏ Dessert ❏ Other

COLOR:

AROMAS:

DRY/SWEET: ❏ Bone-dry ❏ Dry ❏ Off-dry
❏ Medium-sweet ❏ Sweet

TANNINS: ❑ Low (easy to drink) ❑ Medium (balanced)
❑ High (bitter)

ACIDITY: ❑ Flat (very low) ❑ Soft (low)
❑ Balanced ❑ High (lively) ❑ Very high (bracing)

BODY: ❑ Light ❑ Medium ❑ Full

TEXTURE: ❑ Smooth ❑ Light ❑ Prickly/acidic
❑ Balanced ❑ Rough

TASTE:

_____

FINISH: ❑ Short ❑ Medium ❑ Long

FOOD PAIRED WITH IT:

_____

PAIRING SUCCESS: ❑ Disaster ❑ Okay, but not great
❑ Pretty good ❑ Fantastic

ADDITIONAL COMMENTS:

_____

_____

_____

YOUR RATING:
☆ ☆☆ ☆☆☆ ☆☆☆☆ ☆☆☆☆☆

WINE:

PRODUCER:

| **VINTAGE:** | **ALCOHOL %:** | **PRICE:** |

REGION/COUNTRY:

GRAPE(S):

PLACE AND DATE PURCHASED:

| **DATE TASTED:** | **IMPORTER/DISTRIBUTOR:** |

COLOR/STYLE: ❑ Red ❑ White ❑ Rosé
❑ Sparkling ❑ Dessert ❑ Other

COLOR:

AROMAS:

DRY/SWEET: ❑ Bone-dry ❑ Dry ❑ Off-dry
❑ Medium-sweet ❑ Sweet

TANNINS: ❑ Low (easy to drink) ❑ Medium (balanced)
❑ High (bitter)

ACIDITY: ❑ Flat (very low) ❑ Soft (low)
❑ Balanced ❑ High (lively) ❑ Very high (bracing)

BODY: ❑ Light ❑ Medium ❑ Full

TEXTURE: ❑ Smooth ❑ Light ❑ Prickly/acidic
❑ Balanced ❑ Rough

TASTE:

FINISH: ❑ Short ❑ Medium ❑ Long

FOOD PAIRED WITH IT:

PAIRING SUCCESS: ❑ Disaster ❑ Okay, but not great
❑ Pretty good ❑ Fantastic

ADDITIONAL COMMENTS:

YOUR RATING:
☆   ☆☆   ☆☆☆   ☆☆☆☆   ☆☆☆☆☆

WINE:

_____

PRODUCER:

_____

VINTAGE: | ALCOHOL %: | PRICE:

_____

REGION/COUNTRY:

_____

GRAPE(S):

_____

PLACE AND DATE PURCHASED:

_____

DATE TASTED: | IMPORTER/DISTRIBUTOR:

_____

COLOR/STYLE: ❑ Red   ❑ White   ❑ Rosé
❑ Sparkling   ❑ Dessert   ❑ Other

COLOR:

_____

AROMAS:

_____

DRY/SWEET: ❑ Bone-dry   ❑ Dry   ❑ Off-dry
❑ Medium-sweet   ❑ Sweet

TANNINS: ❏ Low (easy to drink) ❏ Medium (balanced)
❏ High (bitter)

ACIDITY: ❏ Flat (very low) ❏ Soft (low)
❏ Balanced ❏ High (lively) ❏ Very high (bracing)

BODY: ❏ Light ❏ Medium ❏ Full

TEXTURE: ❏ Smooth ❏ Light ❏ Prickly/acidic
❏ Balanced ❏ Rough

TASTE:

_____

FINISH: ❏ Short ❏ Medium ❏ Long

FOOD PAIRED WITH IT:

_____

PAIRING SUCCESS: ❏ Disaster ❏ Okay, but not great
❏ Pretty good ❏ Fantastic

ADDITIONAL COMMENTS:

_____

_____

_____

YOUR RATING:
☆　　☆☆　　☆☆☆　　☆☆☆☆　　☆☆☆☆☆

WINE:

_____

PRODUCER:

_____

| VINTAGE: | ALCOHOL %: | PRICE: |

REGION/COUNTRY:

_____

GRAPE(S):

_____

PLACE AND DATE PURCHASED:

_____

| DATE TASTED: | IMPORTER/DISTRIBUTOR: |

COLOR/STYLE: ❑ Red   ❑ White   ❑ Rosé
❑ Sparkling   ❑ Dessert   ❑ Other

COLOR:

_____

AROMAS:

_____

DRY/SWEET: ❑ Bone-dry   ❑ Dry   ❑ Off-dry
❑ Medium-sweet   ❑ Sweet

TANNINS: ❑ Low (easy to drink)   ❑ Medium (balanced)
❑ High (bitter)

ACIDITY: ❑ Flat (very low)   ❑ Soft (low)
❑ Balanced   ❑ High (lively)   ❑ Very high (bracing)

BODY: ❑ Light   ❑ Medium   ❑ Full

TEXTURE: ❑ Smooth   ❑ Light   ❑ Prickly/acidic
❑ Balanced   ❑ Rough

TASTE:

_____

FINISH: ❑ Short   ❑ Medium   ❑ Long

FOOD PAIRED WITH IT:

_____

PAIRING SUCCESS: ❑ Disaster   ❑ Okay, but not great
❑ Pretty good   ❑ Fantastic

ADDITIONAL COMMENTS:

_____

_____

_____

YOUR RATING:
☆   ☆☆   ☆☆☆   ☆☆☆☆   ☆☆☆☆☆

WINE:

PRODUCER:

| VINTAGE: | ALCOHOL %: | PRICE: |

REGION/COUNTRY:

GRAPE(S):

PLACE AND DATE PURCHASED:

| DATE TASTED: | IMPORTER/DISTRIBUTOR: |

COLOR/STYLE: ❑ Red   ❑ White   ❑ Rosé
❑ Sparkling   ❑ Dessert   ❑ Other

COLOR:

AROMAS:

DRY/SWEET: ❑ Bone-dry   ❑ Dry   ❑ Off-dry
❑ Medium-sweet   ❑ Sweet

TANNINS: ❑ Low (easy to drink)   ❑ Medium (balanced)
❑ High (bitter)

ACIDITY: ❑ Flat (very low)   ❑ Soft (low)
❑ Balanced   ❑ High (lively)   ❑ Very high (bracing)

BODY: ❑ Light   ❑ Medium   ❑ Full

TEXTURE: ❑ Smooth   ❑ Light   ❑ Prickly/acidic
❑ Balanced   ❑ Rough

TASTE:

_____

FINISH: ❑ Short   ❑ Medium   ❑ Long

FOOD PAIRED WITH IT:

_____

PAIRING SUCCESS: ❑ Disaster   ❑ Okay, but not great
❑ Pretty good   ❑ Fantastic

ADDITIONAL COMMENTS:

_____

_____

_____

YOUR RATING:
☆   ☆☆   ☆☆☆   ☆☆☆☆   ☆☆☆☆☆

WINE:

_____

PRODUCER:

_____

VINTAGE: | ALCOHOL %: | PRICE:

_____

REGION/COUNTRY:

_____

GRAPE(S):

_____

PLACE AND DATE PURCHASED:

_____

DATE TASTED: | IMPORTER/DISTRIBUTOR:

_____

COLOR/STYLE: ❑ Red ❑ White ❑ Rosé
❑ Sparkling ❑ Dessert ❑ Other

COLOR:

_____

AROMAS:

_____

DRY/SWEET: ❑ Bone-dry ❑ Dry ❑ Off-dry
❑ Medium-sweet ❑ Sweet

TANNINS: ❑ Low (easy to drink)   ❑ Medium (balanced)
❑ High (bitter)

ACIDITY: ❑ Flat (very low)   ❑ Soft (low)
❑ Balanced   ❑ High (lively)   ❑ Very high (bracing)

BODY: ❑ Light   ❑ Medium   ❑ Full

TEXTURE: ❑ Smooth   ❑ Light   ❑ Prickly/acidic
❑ Balanced   ❑ Rough

TASTE:

_____

FINISH: ❑ Short   ❑ Medium   ❑ Long

FOOD PAIRED WITH IT:

_____

PAIRING SUCCESS: ❑ Disaster   ❑ Okay, but not great
❑ Pretty good   ❑ Fantastic

ADDITIONAL COMMENTS:

_____

_____

_____

YOUR RATING:
☆   ☆☆   ☆☆☆   ☆☆☆☆   ☆☆☆☆☆

WINE:

_____

PRODUCER:

_____

VINTAGE:	ALCOHOL %:	PRICE:

REGION/COUNTRY:

_____

GRAPE(S):

_____

PLACE AND DATE PURCHASED:

_____

DATE TASTED:	IMPORTER/DISTRIBUTOR:

COLOR/STYLE: ❏ Red ❏ White ❏ Rosé
❏ Sparkling ❏ Dessert ❏ Other

COLOR:

_____

AROMAS:

_____

DRY/SWEET: ❏ Bone-dry ❏ Dry ❏ Off-dry
❏ Medium-sweet ❏ Sweet

TANNINS: ❑ Low (easy to drink)   ❑ Medium (balanced)
❑ High (bitter)

ACIDITY: ❑ Flat (very low)   ❑ Soft (low)
❑ Balanced   ❑ High (lively)   ❑ Very high (bracing)

BODY: ❑ Light   ❑ Medium   ❑ Full

TEXTURE: ❑ Smooth   ❑ Light   ❑ Prickly/acidic
❑ Balanced   ❑ Rough

TASTE:

_____

FINISH: ❑ Short   ❑ Medium   ❑ Long

FOOD PAIRED WITH IT:

_____

PAIRING SUCCESS: ❑ Disaster   ❑ Okay, but not great
❑ Pretty good   ❑ Fantastic

ADDITIONAL COMMENTS:

_____

_____

_____

YOUR RATING:
☆   ☆☆   ☆☆☆   ☆☆☆☆   ☆☆☆☆☆

WINE:

_____

PRODUCER:

_____

| VINTAGE: | ALCOHOL %: | PRICE: |

_____

REGION/COUNTRY:

_____

GRAPE(S):

_____

PLACE AND DATE PURCHASED:

_____

| DATE TASTED: | IMPORTER/DISTRIBUTOR: |

_____

COLOR/STYLE: ❑ Red ❑ White ❑ Rosé
❑ Sparkling ❑ Dessert ❑ Other

COLOR:

_____

AROMAS:

_____

DRY/SWEET: ❑ Bone-dry ❑ Dry ❑ Off-dry
❑ Medium-sweet ❑ Sweet

TANNINS: ❑ Low (easy to drink)   ❑ Medium (balanced)
❑ High (bitter)

ACIDITY: ❑ Flat (very low)   ❑ Soft (low)
❑ Balanced   ❑ High (lively)   ❑ Very high (bracing)

BODY: ❑ Light   ❑ Medium   ❑ Full

TEXTURE: ❑ Smooth   ❑ Light   ❑ Prickly/acidic
❑ Balanced   ❑ Rough

TASTE:

FINISH: ❑ Short   ❑ Medium   ❑ Long

FOOD PAIRED WITH IT:

PAIRING SUCCESS: ❑ Disaster   ❑ Okay, but not great
❑ Pretty good   ❑ Fantastic

ADDITIONAL COMMENTS:

YOUR RATING:
☆   ☆☆   ☆☆☆   ☆☆☆☆   ☆☆☆☆☆

WINE:

_____

PRODUCER:

_____

| VINTAGE: | ALCOHOL %: | PRICE: |

REGION/COUNTRY:

_____

GRAPE(S):

_____

PLACE AND DATE PURCHASED:

_____

| DATE TASTED: | IMPORTER/DISTRIBUTOR: |

COLOR/STYLE: ❑ Red   ❑ White   ❑ Rosé
❑ Sparkling   ❑ Dessert   ❑ Other

COLOR:

_____

AROMAS:

_____

DRY/SWEET: ❑ Bone-dry   ❑ Dry   ❑ Off-dry
❑ Medium-sweet   ❑ Sweet

TANNINS: ❏ Low (easy to drink) ❏ Medium (balanced)
❏ High (bitter)

ACIDITY: ❏ Flat (very low) ❏ Soft (low)
❏ Balanced ❏ High (lively) ❏ Very high (bracing)

BODY: ❏ Light ❏ Medium ❏ Full

TEXTURE: ❏ Smooth ❏ Light ❏ Prickly/acidic
❏ Balanced ❏ Rough

TASTE:

FINISH: ❏ Short ❏ Medium ❏ Long

FOOD PAIRED WITH IT:

PAIRING SUCCESS: ❏ Disaster ❏ Okay, but not great
❏ Pretty good ❏ Fantastic

ADDITIONAL COMMENTS:

YOUR RATING:
☆   ☆☆   ☆☆☆   ☆☆☆☆   ☆☆☆☆☆

WINE:

_____

PRODUCER:

_____

VINTAGE:	ALCOHOL %:	PRICE:

REGION/COUNTRY:

_____

GRAPE(S):

_____

PLACE AND DATE PURCHASED:

_____

DATE TASTED:	IMPORTER/DISTRIBUTOR:

COLOR/STYLE: ❑ Red   ❑ White   ❑ Rosé
❑ Sparkling   ❑ Dessert   ❑ Other

COLOR:

_____

AROMAS:

_____

DRY/SWEET: ❑ Bone-dry   ❑ Dry   ❑ Off-dry
❑ Medium-sweet   ❑ Sweet

TANNINS: ❑ Low (easy to drink)   ❑ Medium (balanced)
❑ High (bitter)

ACIDITY: ❑ Flat (very low)   ❑ Soft (low)
❑ Balanced   ❑ High (lively)   ❑ Very high (bracing)

BODY: ❑ Light   ❑ Medium   ❑ Full

TEXTURE: ❑ Smooth   ❑ Light   ❑ Prickly/acidic
❑ Balanced   ❑ Rough

TASTE:

_____

FINISH: ❑ Short   ❑ Medium   ❑ Long

FOOD PAIRED WITH IT:

_____

PAIRING SUCCESS: ❑ Disaster   ❑ Okay, but not great
❑ Pretty good   ❑ Fantastic

ADDITIONAL COMMENTS:

_____

_____

_____

YOUR RATING:
☆   ☆☆   ☆☆☆   ☆☆☆☆   ☆☆☆☆☆

WINE:

PRODUCER:

| **VINTAGE:** | **ALCOHOL %:** | **PRICE:** |

REGION/COUNTRY:

GRAPE(S):

PLACE AND DATE PURCHASED:

| **DATE TASTED:** | **IMPORTER/DISTRIBUTOR:** |

COLOR/STYLE: ❑ Red ❑ White ❑ Rosé
❑ Sparkling ❑ Dessert ❑ Other

COLOR:

AROMAS:

DRY/SWEET: ❑ Bone-dry ❑ Dry ❑ Off-dry
❑ Medium-sweet ❑ Sweet

TANNINS: ❑ Low (easy to drink)   ❑ Medium (balanced)
❑ High (bitter)

ACIDITY: ❑ Flat (very low)   ❑ Soft (low)
❑ Balanced   ❑ High (lively)   ❑ Very high (bracing)

BODY: ❑ Light   ❑ Medium   ❑ Full

TEXTURE: ❑ Smooth   ❑ Light   ❑ Prickly/acidic
❑ Balanced   ❑ Rough

TASTE:

FINISH: ❑ Short   ❑ Medium   ❑ Long

FOOD PAIRED WITH IT:

PAIRING SUCCESS: ❑ Disaster   ❑ Okay, but not great
❑ Pretty good   ❑ Fantastic

ADDITIONAL COMMENTS:

YOUR RATING:
☆   ☆☆   ☆☆☆   ☆☆☆☆   ☆☆☆☆☆

WINE:

_____

PRODUCER:

_____

VINTAGE: | ALCOHOL %: | PRICE:

_____

REGION/COUNTRY:

_____

GRAPE(S):

_____

PLACE AND DATE PURCHASED:

_____

DATE TASTED: | IMPORTER/DISTRIBUTOR:

_____

COLOR/STYLE: ❑ Red ❑ White ❑ Rosé
❑ Sparkling ❑ Dessert ❑ Other

COLOR:

_____

AROMAS:

_____

DRY/SWEET: ❑ Bone-dry ❑ Dry ❑ Off-dry
❑ Medium-sweet ❑ Sweet

TANNINS: ❑ Low (easy to drink)   ❑ Medium (balanced)
❑ High (bitter)

ACIDITY: ❑ Flat (very low)   ❑ Soft (low)
❑ Balanced   ❑ High (lively)   ❑ Very high (bracing)

BODY: ❑ Light   ❑ Medium   ❑ Full

TEXTURE: ❑ Smooth   ❑ Light   ❑ Prickly/acidic
❑ Balanced   ❑ Rough

TASTE:

_____

FINISH: ❑ Short   ❑ Medium   ❑ Long

FOOD PAIRED WITH IT:

_____

PAIRING SUCCESS: ❑ Disaster   ❑ Okay, but not great
❑ Pretty good   ❑ Fantastic

ADDITIONAL COMMENTS:

_____

_____

_____

YOUR RATING:
☆   ☆☆   ☆☆☆   ☆☆☆☆   ☆☆☆☆☆

WINE:

PRODUCER:

| VINTAGE: | ALCOHOL %: | PRICE: |

REGION/COUNTRY:

GRAPE(S):

PLACE AND DATE PURCHASED:

| DATE TASTED: | IMPORTER/DISTRIBUTOR: |

COLOR/STYLE:　❑ Red　　❑ White　　❑ Rosé
❑ Sparkling　　❑ Dessert　　❑ Other

COLOR:

AROMAS:

DRY/SWEET:　❑ Bone-dry　　❑ Dry　　❑ Off-dry
❑ Medium-sweet　　❑ Sweet

TANNINS: ❑ Low (easy to drink)   ❑ Medium (balanced)
❑ High (bitter)

ACIDITY: ❑ Flat (very low)   ❑ Soft (low)
❑ Balanced   ❑ High (lively)   ❑ Very high (bracing)

BODY: ❑ Light   ❑ Medium   ❑ Full

TEXTURE: ❑ Smooth   ❑ Light   ❑ Prickly/acidic
❑ Balanced   ❑ Rough

TASTE:

_____

FINISH: ❑ Short   ❑ Medium   ❑ Long

FOOD PAIRED WITH IT:

_____

PAIRING SUCCESS: ❑ Disaster   ❑ Okay, but not great
❑ Pretty good   ❑ Fantastic

ADDITIONAL COMMENTS:

_____

_____

_____

YOUR RATING:
☆   ☆☆   ☆☆☆   ☆☆☆☆   ☆☆☆☆☆

WINE:

_____

PRODUCER:

_____

VINTAGE:	ALCOHOL %:	PRICE:

REGION/COUNTRY:

_____

GRAPE(S):

_____

PLACE AND DATE PURCHASED:

_____

DATE TASTED:	IMPORTER/DISTRIBUTOR:

COLOR/STYLE: ❑ Red   ❑ White   ❑ Rosé
❑ Sparkling   ❑ Dessert   ❑ Other

COLOR:

_____

AROMAS:

_____

DRY/SWEET: ❑ Bone-dry   ❑ Dry   ❑ Off-dry
❑ Medium-sweet   ❑ Sweet

TANNINS: ❑ Low (easy to drink)   ❑ Medium (balanced)
❑ High (bitter)

ACIDITY: ❑ Flat (very low)   ❑ Soft (low)
❑ Balanced   ❑ High (lively)   ❑ Very high (bracing)

BODY: ❑ Light   ❑ Medium   ❑ Full

TEXTURE: ❑ Smooth   ❑ Light   ❑ Prickly/acidic
❑ Balanced   ❑ Rough

TASTE:

_____

FINISH: ❑ Short   ❑ Medium   ❑ Long

FOOD PAIRED WITH IT:

_____

PAIRING SUCCESS: ❑ Disaster   ❑ Okay, but not great
❑ Pretty good   ❑ Fantastic

ADDITIONAL COMMENTS:

_____

_____

_____

YOUR RATING:
☆   ☆☆   ☆☆☆   ☆☆☆☆   ☆☆☆☆☆

WINE:

_____

PRODUCER:

_____

VINTAGE: | ALCOHOL %: | PRICE:

_____

REGION/COUNTRY:

_____

GRAPE(S):

_____

PLACE AND DATE PURCHASED:

_____

DATE TASTED: | IMPORTER/DISTRIBUTOR:

_____

COLOR/STYLE: ❑ Red ❑ White ❑ Rosé
❑ Sparkling ❑ Dessert ❑ Other

COLOR:

_____

AROMAS:

_____

DRY/SWEET: ❑ Bone-dry ❑ Dry ❑ Off-dry
❑ Medium-sweet ❑ Sweet

TANNINS: ❑ Low (easy to drink)   ❑ Medium (balanced)
❑ High (bitter)

ACIDITY: ❑ Flat (very low)   ❑ Soft (low)
❑ Balanced   ❑ High (lively)   ❑ Very high (bracing)

BODY: ❑ Light   ❑ Medium   ❑ Full

TEXTURE: ❑ Smooth   ❑ Light   ❑ Prickly/acidic
❑ Balanced   ❑ Rough

TASTE:

_____

FINISH: ❑ Short   ❑ Medium   ❑ Long

FOOD PAIRED WITH IT:

_____

PAIRING SUCCESS: ❑ Disaster   ❑ Okay, but not great
❑ Pretty good   ❑ Fantastic

ADDITIONAL COMMENTS:

_____

_____

_____

YOUR RATING:
☆   ☆☆   ☆☆☆   ☆☆☆☆   ☆☆☆☆☆

WINE:

_____

PRODUCER:

_____

VINTAGE: | ALCOHOL %: | PRICE:

_____

REGION/COUNTRY:

_____

GRAPE(S):

_____

PLACE AND DATE PURCHASED:

_____

DATE TASTED: | IMPORTER/DISTRIBUTOR:

_____

COLOR/STYLE: ❑ Red ❑ White ❑ Rosé
❑ Sparkling ❑ Dessert ❑ Other

COLOR:

_____

AROMAS:

_____

DRY/SWEET: ❑ Bone-dry ❑ Dry ❑ Off-dry
❑ Medium-sweet ❑ Sweet

TANNINS: ❏ Low (easy to drink)   ❏ Medium (balanced)
❏ High (bitter)

ACIDITY: ❏ Flat (very low)   ❏ Soft (low)
❏ Balanced   ❏ High (lively)   ❏ Very high (bracing)

BODY: ❏ Light   ❏ Medium   ❏ Full

TEXTURE: ❏ Smooth   ❏ Light   ❏ Prickly/acidic
❏ Balanced   ❏ Rough

TASTE:

FINISH: ❏ Short   ❏ Medium   ❏ Long

FOOD PAIRED WITH IT:

PAIRING SUCCESS: ❏ Disaster   ❏ Okay, but not great
❏ Pretty good   ❏ Fantastic

ADDITIONAL COMMENTS:

YOUR RATING:
☆   ☆☆   ☆☆☆   ☆☆☆☆   ☆☆☆☆☆

WINE:

PRODUCER:

| **VINTAGE:** | **ALCOHOL %:** | **PRICE:** |

REGION/COUNTRY:

GRAPE(S):

PLACE AND DATE PURCHASED:

| **DATE TASTED:** | **IMPORTER/DISTRIBUTOR:** |

COLOR/STYLE: ❑ Red ❑ White ❑ Rosé
❑ Sparkling ❑ Dessert ❑ Other

COLOR:

AROMAS:

DRY/SWEET: ❑ Bone-dry ❑ Dry ❑ Off-dry
❑ Medium-sweet ❑ Sweet

TANNINS: ❑ Low (easy to drink)   ❑ Medium (balanced)
❑ High (bitter)

ACIDITY: ❑ Flat (very low)   ❑ Soft (low)
❑ Balanced   ❑ High (lively)   ❑ Very high (bracing)

BODY: ❑ Light   ❑ Medium   ❑ Full

TEXTURE: ❑ Smooth   ❑ Light   ❑ Prickly/acidic
❑ Balanced   ❑ Rough

TASTE:

FINISH: ❑ Short   ❑ Medium   ❑ Long

FOOD PAIRED WITH IT:

PAIRING SUCCESS: ❑ Disaster   ❑ Okay, but not great
❑ Pretty good   ❑ Fantastic

ADDITIONAL COMMENTS:

YOUR RATING:
☆   ☆☆   ☆☆☆   ☆☆☆☆   ☆☆☆☆☆

WINE:

_____

PRODUCER:

_____

| VINTAGE: | ALCOHOL %: | PRICE: |

_____

REGION/COUNTRY:

_____

GRAPE(S):

_____

PLACE AND DATE PURCHASED:

_____

DATE TASTED: | IMPORTER/DISTRIBUTOR:

_____

COLOR/STYLE: ❑ Red ❑ White ❑ Rosé
❑ Sparkling ❑ Dessert ❑ Other

COLOR:

_____

AROMAS:

_____

DRY/SWEET: ❑ Bone-dry ❑ Dry ❑ Off-dry
❑ Medium-sweet ❑ Sweet

TANNINS: ❏ Low (easy to drink)   ❏ Medium (balanced)
❏ High (bitter)

ACIDITY: ❏ Flat (very low)   ❏ Soft (low)
❏ Balanced   ❏ High (lively)   ❏ Very high (bracing)

BODY: ❏ Light   ❏ Medium   ❏ Full

TEXTURE: ❏ Smooth   ❏ Light   ❏ Prickly/acidic
❏ Balanced   ❏ Rough

TASTE:

FINISH: ❏ Short   ❏ Medium   ❏ Long

FOOD PAIRED WITH IT:

PAIRING SUCCESS: ❏ Disaster   ❏ Okay, but not great
❏ Pretty good   ❏ Fantastic

ADDITIONAL COMMENTS:

YOUR RATING:
☆   ☆☆   ☆☆☆   ☆☆☆☆   ☆☆☆☆☆

WINE:

PRODUCER:

| VINTAGE: | ALCOHOL %: | PRICE: |

REGION/COUNTRY:

GRAPE(S):

PLACE AND DATE PURCHASED:

| DATE TASTED: | IMPORTER/DISTRIBUTOR: |

COLOR/STYLE: ❏ Red   ❏ White   ❏ Rosé
❏ Sparkling   ❏ Dessert   ❏ Other

COLOR:

AROMAS:

DRY/SWEET: ❏ Bone-dry   ❏ Dry   ❏ Off-dry
❏ Medium-sweet   ❏ Sweet

TANNINS: ❑ Low (easy to drink)   ❑ Medium (balanced)
❑ High (bitter)

ACIDITY: ❑ Flat (very low)   ❑ Soft (low)
❑ Balanced   ❑ High (lively)   ❑ Very high (bracing)

BODY: ❑ Light   ❑ Medium   ❑ Full

TEXTURE: ❑ Smooth   ❑ Light   ❑ Prickly/acidic
❑ Balanced   ❑ Rough

TASTE:

_____

FINISH: ❑ Short   ❑ Medium   ❑ Long

FOOD PAIRED WITH IT:

_____

PAIRING SUCCESS: ❑ Disaster   ❑ Okay, but not great
❑ Pretty good   ❑ Fantastic

ADDITIONAL COMMENTS:

_____

_____

_____

YOUR RATING:
☆   ☆☆   ☆☆☆   ☆☆☆☆   ☆☆☆☆☆

WINE:

___

PRODUCER:

___

VINTAGE: | ALCOHOL %: | PRICE:

___

REGION/COUNTRY:

___

GRAPE(S):

___

PLACE AND DATE PURCHASED:

___

DATE TASTED: | IMPORTER/DISTRIBUTOR:

___

COLOR/STYLE: ❑ Red ❑ White ❑ Rosé
❑ Sparkling ❑ Dessert ❑ Other

COLOR:

___

AROMAS:

___

DRY/SWEET: ❑ Bone-dry ❑ Dry ❑ Off-dry
❑ Medium-sweet ❑ Sweet

TANNINS: ❑ Low (easy to drink) ❑ Medium (balanced)
❑ High (bitter)

ACIDITY: ❑ Flat (very low) ❑ Soft (low)
❑ Balanced ❑ High (lively) ❑ Very high (bracing)

BODY: ❑ Light ❑ Medium ❑ Full

TEXTURE: ❑ Smooth ❑ Light ❑ Prickly/acidic
❑ Balanced ❑ Rough

TASTE:

FINISH: ❑ Short ❑ Medium ❑ Long

FOOD PAIRED WITH IT:

PAIRING SUCCESS: ❑ Disaster ❑ Okay, but not great
❑ Pretty good ❑ Fantastic

ADDITIONAL COMMENTS:

YOUR RATING:
☆   ☆☆   ☆☆☆   ☆☆☆☆   ☆☆☆☆☆

WINE:

_____

PRODUCER:

_____

VINTAGE: | ALCOHOL %: | PRICE:

_____

REGION/COUNTRY:

_____

GRAPE(S):

_____

PLACE AND DATE PURCHASED:

_____

DATE TASTED: | IMPORTER/DISTRIBUTOR:

_____

COLOR/STYLE: ❑ Red ❑ White ❑ Rosé
❑ Sparkling ❑ Dessert ❑ Other

COLOR:

_____

AROMAS:

_____

DRY/SWEET: ❑ Bone-dry ❑ Dry ❑ Off-dry
❑ Medium-sweet ❑ Sweet

TANNINS: ❑ Low (easy to drink) ❑ Medium (balanced)
❑ High (bitter)

ACIDITY: ❑ Flat (very low) ❑ Soft (low)
❑ Balanced ❑ High (lively) ❑ Very high (bracing)

BODY: ❑ Light ❑ Medium ❑ Full

TEXTURE: ❑ Smooth ❑ Light ❑ Prickly/acidic
❑ Balanced ❑ Rough

TASTE:

_____

FINISH: ❑ Short ❑ Medium ❑ Long

FOOD PAIRED WITH IT:

_____

PAIRING SUCCESS: ❑ Disaster ❑ Okay, but not great
❑ Pretty good ❑ Fantastic

ADDITIONAL COMMENTS:

_____

_____

_____

YOUR RATING:
☆ ☆☆ ☆☆☆ ☆☆☆☆ ☆☆☆☆☆

WINE:

PRODUCER:

| VINTAGE: | ALCOHOL %: | PRICE: |

REGION/COUNTRY:

GRAPE(S):

PLACE AND DATE PURCHASED:

| DATE TASTED: | IMPORTER/DISTRIBUTOR: |

COLOR/STYLE: ❑ Red ❑ White ❑ Rosé
❑ Sparkling ❑ Dessert ❑ Other

COLOR:

AROMAS:

DRY/SWEET: ❑ Bone-dry ❑ Dry ❑ Off-dry
❑ Medium-sweet ❑ Sweet

TANNINS: ❑ Low (easy to drink)　❑ Medium (balanced)
❑ High (bitter)

ACIDITY: ❑ Flat (very low)　❑ Soft (low)
❑ Balanced　❑ High (lively)　❑ Very high (bracing)

BODY: ❑ Light　❑ Medium　❑ Full

TEXTURE: ❑ Smooth　❑ Light　❑ Prickly/acidic
❑ Balanced　❑ Rough

TASTE:

_____

FINISH: ❑ Short　❑ Medium　❑ Long

FOOD PAIRED WITH IT:

_____

PAIRING SUCCESS: ❑ Disaster　❑ Okay, but not great
❑ Pretty good　❑ Fantastic

ADDITIONAL COMMENTS:

_____

_____

_____

YOUR RATING:
☆　　☆☆　　☆☆☆　　☆☆☆☆　　☆☆☆☆☆

WINE:

PRODUCER:

VINTAGE: | ALCOHOL %: | PRICE:

REGION/COUNTRY:

GRAPE(S):

PLACE AND DATE PURCHASED:

DATE TASTED: | IMPORTER/DISTRIBUTOR:

COLOR/STYLE: ❑ Red ❑ White ❑ Rosé
❑ Sparkling ❑ Dessert ❑ Other

COLOR:

AROMAS:

DRY/SWEET: ❑ Bone-dry ❑ Dry ❑ Off-dry
❑ Medium-sweet ❑ Sweet

TANNINS: ❑ Low (easy to drink)   ❑ Medium (balanced)
❑ High (bitter)

ACIDITY: ❑ Flat (very low)   ❑ Soft (low)
❑ Balanced   ❑ High (lively)   ❑ Very high (bracing)

BODY: ❑ Light   ❑ Medium   ❑ Full

TEXTURE: ❑ Smooth   ❑ Light   ❑ Prickly/acidic
❑ Balanced   ❑ Rough

TASTE:

FINISH: ❑ Short   ❑ Medium   ❑ Long

FOOD PAIRED WITH IT:

PAIRING SUCCESS: ❑ Disaster   ❑ Okay, but not great
❑ Pretty good   ❑ Fantastic

ADDITIONAL COMMENTS:

YOUR RATING:
☆   ☆☆   ☆☆☆   ☆☆☆☆   ☆☆☆☆☆

WINE:

PRODUCER:

| VINTAGE: | ALCOHOL %: | PRICE: |

REGION/COUNTRY:

GRAPE(S):

PLACE AND DATE PURCHASED:

| DATE TASTED: | IMPORTER/DISTRIBUTOR: |

COLOR/STYLE: ❏ Red ❏ White ❏ Rosé
❏ Sparkling ❏ Dessert ❏ Other

COLOR:

AROMAS:

DRY/SWEET: ❏ Bone-dry ❏ Dry ❏ Off-dry
❏ Medium-sweet ❏ Sweet

TANNINS: ❑ Low (easy to drink) ❑ Medium (balanced)
❑ High (bitter)

ACIDITY: ❑ Flat (very low) ❑ Soft (low)
❑ Balanced ❑ High (lively) ❑ Very high (bracing)

BODY: ❑ Light ❑ Medium ❑ Full

TEXTURE: ❑ Smooth ❑ Light ❑ Prickly/acidic
❑ Balanced ❑ Rough

TASTE:

_____

FINISH: ❑ Short ❑ Medium ❑ Long

FOOD PAIRED WITH IT:

_____

PAIRING SUCCESS: ❑ Disaster ❑ Okay, but not great
❑ Pretty good ❑ Fantastic

ADDITIONAL COMMENTS:

_____

_____

_____

YOUR RATING:
☆ ☆☆ ☆☆☆ ☆☆☆☆ ☆☆☆☆☆

WINE:

PRODUCER:

| VINTAGE: | ALCOHOL %: | PRICE: |

REGION/COUNTRY:

GRAPE(S):

PLACE AND DATE PURCHASED:

| DATE TASTED: | IMPORTER/DISTRIBUTOR: |

COLOR/STYLE: ❏ Red   ❏ White   ❏ Rosé
❏ Sparkling   ❏ Dessert   ❏ Other

COLOR:

AROMAS:

DRY/SWEET: ❏ Bone-dry   ❏ Dry   ❏ Off-dry
❏ Medium-sweet   ❏ Sweet

TANNINS: ❑ Low (easy to drink)   ❑ Medium (balanced)
❑ High (bitter)

ACIDITY: ❑ Flat (very low)   ❑ Soft (low)
❑ Balanced   ❑ High (lively)   ❑ Very high (bracing)

BODY: ❑ Light   ❑ Medium   ❑ Full

TEXTURE: ❑ Smooth   ❑ Light   ❑ Prickly/acidic
❑ Balanced   ❑ Rough

TASTE:

_____

FINISH: ❑ Short   ❑ Medium   ❑ Long

FOOD PAIRED WITH IT:

_____

PAIRING SUCCESS: ❑ Disaster   ❑ Okay, but not great
❑ Pretty good   ❑ Fantastic

ADDITIONAL COMMENTS:

_____

_____

_____

YOUR RATING:
☆   ☆☆   ☆☆☆   ☆☆☆☆   ☆☆☆☆☆

WINE:

_____

PRODUCER:

_____

| VINTAGE: | ALCOHOL %: | PRICE: |

REGION/COUNTRY:

_____

GRAPE(S):

_____

PLACE AND DATE PURCHASED:

_____

| DATE TASTED: | IMPORTER/DISTRIBUTOR: |

COLOR/STYLE: ❑ Red ❑ White ❑ Rosé
❑ Sparkling ❑ Dessert ❑ Other

COLOR:

_____

AROMAS:

_____

DRY/SWEET: ❑ Bone-dry ❑ Dry ❑ Off-dry
❑ Medium-sweet ❑ Sweet

TANNINS: ❑ Low (easy to drink)   ❑ Medium (balanced)
❑ High (bitter)

ACIDITY: ❑ Flat (very low)   ❑ Soft (low)
❑ Balanced   ❑ High (lively)   ❑ Very high (bracing)

BODY: ❑ Light   ❑ Medium   ❑ Full

TEXTURE: ❑ Smooth   ❑ Light   ❑ Prickly/acidic
❑ Balanced   ❑ Rough

TASTE:

_____

FINISH: ❑ Short   ❑ Medium   ❑ Long

FOOD PAIRED WITH IT:

_____

PAIRING SUCCESS: ❑ Disaster   ❑ Okay, but not great
❑ Pretty good   ❑ Fantastic

ADDITIONAL COMMENTS:

_____

_____

_____

YOUR RATING:
☆   ☆☆   ☆☆☆   ☆☆☆☆   ☆☆☆☆☆

WINE:

PRODUCER:

VINTAGE: | **ALCOHOL %:** | **PRICE:**

REGION/COUNTRY:

GRAPE(S):

PLACE AND DATE PURCHASED:

DATE TASTED: | **IMPORTER/DISTRIBUTOR:**

COLOR/STYLE: ❑ Red ❑ White ❑ Rosé
❑ Sparkling ❑ Dessert ❑ Other

COLOR:

AROMAS:

DRY/SWEET: ❑ Bone-dry ❑ Dry ❑ Off-dry
❑ Medium-sweet ❑ Sweet

TANNINS: ❑ Low (easy to drink)   ❑ Medium (balanced)
❑ High (bitter)

ACIDITY: ❑ Flat (very low)   ❑ Soft (low)
❑ Balanced   ❑ High (lively)   ❑ Very high (bracing)

BODY: ❑ Light   ❑ Medium   ❑ Full

TEXTURE: ❑ Smooth   ❑ Light   ❑ Prickly/acidic
❑ Balanced   ❑ Rough

TASTE:

_____

FINISH: ❑ Short   ❑ Medium   ❑ Long

FOOD PAIRED WITH IT:

_____

PAIRING SUCCESS: ❑ Disaster   ❑ Okay, but not great
❑ Pretty good   ❑ Fantastic

ADDITIONAL COMMENTS:

_____

_____

_____

YOUR RATING:
☆   ☆☆   ☆☆☆   ☆☆☆☆   ☆☆☆☆☆

WINE:

PRODUCER:

| VINTAGE: | ALCOHOL %: | PRICE: |

REGION/COUNTRY:

GRAPE(S):

PLACE AND DATE PURCHASED:

| DATE TASTED: | IMPORTER/DISTRIBUTOR: |

COLOR/STYLE: ❑ Red ❑ White ❑ Rosé
❑ Sparkling ❑ Dessert ❑ Other

COLOR:

AROMAS:

DRY/SWEET: ❑ Bone-dry ❑ Dry ❑ Off-dry
❑ Medium-sweet ❑ Sweet

TANNINS: ❑ Low (easy to drink)   ❑ Medium (balanced)
❑ High (bitter)

ACIDITY: ❑ Flat (very low)   ❑ Soft (low)
❑ Balanced   ❑ High (lively)   ❑ Very high (bracing)

BODY: ❑ Light   ❑ Medium   ❑ Full

TEXTURE: ❑ Smooth   ❑ Light   ❑ Prickly/acidic
❑ Balanced   ❑ Rough

TASTE:

FINISH: ❑ Short   ❑ Medium   ❑ Long

FOOD PAIRED WITH IT:

PAIRING SUCCESS: ❑ Disaster   ❑ Okay, but not great
❑ Pretty good   ❑ Fantastic

ADDITIONAL COMMENTS:

YOUR RATING:
☆   ☆☆   ☆☆☆   ☆☆☆☆   ☆☆☆☆☆

WINE:

_____

PRODUCER:

_____

| VINTAGE: | ALCOHOL %: | PRICE: |

_____

REGION/COUNTRY:

_____

GRAPE(S):

_____

PLACE AND DATE PURCHASED:

_____

| DATE TASTED: | IMPORTER/DISTRIBUTOR: |

_____

COLOR/STYLE: ❑ Red   ❑ White   ❑ Rosé
❑ Sparkling   ❑ Dessert   ❑ Other

COLOR:

_____

AROMAS:

_____

DRY/SWEET: ❑ Bone-dry   ❑ Dry   ❑ Off-dry
❑ Medium-sweet   ❑ Sweet

TANNINS: ❑ Low (easy to drink) ❑ Medium (balanced)
❑ High (bitter)

ACIDITY: ❑ Flat (very low) ❑ Soft (low)
❑ Balanced ❑ High (lively) ❑ Very high (bracing)

BODY: ❑ Light ❑ Medium ❑ Full

TEXTURE: ❑ Smooth ❑ Light ❑ Prickly/acidic
❑ Balanced ❑ Rough

TASTE:

FINISH: ❑ Short ❑ Medium ❑ Long

FOOD PAIRED WITH IT:

PAIRING SUCCESS: ❑ Disaster ❑ Okay, but not great
❑ Pretty good ❑ Fantastic

ADDITIONAL COMMENTS:

YOUR RATING:
☆ ☆☆ ☆☆☆ ☆☆☆☆ ☆☆☆☆☆

WINE:

_____

PRODUCER:

_____

| VINTAGE: | ALCOHOL %: | PRICE: |

_____

REGION/COUNTRY:

_____

GRAPE(S):

_____

PLACE AND DATE PURCHASED:

_____

| DATE TASTED: | IMPORTER/DISTRIBUTOR: |

_____

COLOR/STYLE: ❑ Red   ❑ White   ❑ Rosé
❑ Sparkling   ❑ Dessert   ❑ Other

COLOR:

_____

AROMAS:

_____

DRY/SWEET: ❑ Bone-dry   ❑ Dry   ❑ Off-dry
❑ Medium-sweet   ❑ Sweet

TANNINS: ❏ Low (easy to drink) ❏ Medium (balanced)
❏ High (bitter)

ACIDITY: ❏ Flat (very low) ❏ Soft (low)
❏ Balanced ❏ High (lively) ❏ Very high (bracing)

BODY: ❏ Light ❏ Medium ❏ Full

TEXTURE: ❏ Smooth ❏ Light ❏ Prickly/acidic
❏ Balanced ❏ Rough

TASTE:

FINISH: ❏ Short ❏ Medium ❏ Long

FOOD PAIRED WITH IT:

PAIRING SUCCESS: ❏ Disaster ❏ Okay, but not great
❏ Pretty good ❏ Fantastic

ADDITIONAL COMMENTS:

YOUR RATING:
☆ ☆☆ ☆☆☆ ☆☆☆☆ ☆☆☆☆☆

WINE:

_____

PRODUCER:

_____

| VINTAGE: | ALCOHOL %: | PRICE: |

REGION/COUNTRY:

_____

GRAPE(S):

_____

PLACE AND DATE PURCHASED:

_____

| DATE TASTED: | IMPORTER/DISTRIBUTOR: |

COLOR/STYLE: ❑ Red ❑ White ❑ Rosé
❑ Sparkling ❑ Dessert ❑ Other

COLOR:

_____

AROMAS:

_____

DRY/SWEET: ❑ Bone-dry ❑ Dry ❑ Off-dry
❑ Medium-sweet ❑ Sweet

TANNINS: ❑ Low (easy to drink)   ❑ Medium (balanced)
❑ High (bitter)

ACIDITY: ❑ Flat (very low)   ❑ Soft (low)
❑ Balanced   ❑ High (lively)   ❑ Very high (bracing)

BODY: ❑ Light   ❑ Medium   ❑ Full

TEXTURE: ❑ Smooth   ❑ Light   ❑ Prickly/acidic
❑ Balanced   ❑ Rough

TASTE:

FINISH: ❑ Short   ❑ Medium   ❑ Long

FOOD PAIRED WITH IT:

PAIRING SUCCESS: ❑ Disaster   ❑ Okay, but not great
❑ Pretty good   ❑ Fantastic

ADDITIONAL COMMENTS:

YOUR RATING:
☆   ☆☆   ☆☆☆   ☆☆☆☆   ☆☆☆☆☆

WINE:

_____

PRODUCER:

_____

| VINTAGE: | ALCOHOL %: | PRICE: |

_____

REGION/COUNTRY:

_____

GRAPE(S):

_____

PLACE AND DATE PURCHASED:

_____

| DATE TASTED: | IMPORTER/DISTRIBUTOR: |

_____

COLOR/STYLE: ❑ Red ❑ White ❑ Rosé
❑ Sparkling ❑ Dessert ❑ Other

COLOR:

_____

AROMAS:

_____

DRY/SWEET: ❑ Bone-dry ❑ Dry ❑ Off-dry
❑ Medium-sweet ❑ Sweet

TANNINS: ❑ Low (easy to drink) ❑ Medium (balanced)
❑ High (bitter)

ACIDITY: ❑ Flat (very low) ❑ Soft (low)
❑ Balanced ❑ High (lively) ❑ Very high (bracing)

BODY: ❑ Light ❑ Medium ❑ Full

TEXTURE: ❑ Smooth ❑ Light ❑ Prickly/acidic
❑ Balanced ❑ Rough

TASTE:

_____

FINISH: ❑ Short ❑ Medium ❑ Long

FOOD PAIRED WITH IT:

_____

PAIRING SUCCESS: ❑ Disaster ❑ Okay, but not great
❑ Pretty good ❑ Fantastic

ADDITIONAL COMMENTS:

_____

_____

_____

YOUR RATING:
☆ ☆☆ ☆☆☆ ☆☆☆☆ ☆☆☆☆☆

WINE:

_____

PRODUCER:

_____

VINTAGE: | ALCOHOL %: | PRICE:

_____

REGION/COUNTRY:

_____

GRAPE(S):

_____

PLACE AND DATE PURCHASED:

_____

DATE TASTED: | IMPORTER/DISTRIBUTOR:

_____

COLOR/STYLE: ❑ Red ❑ White ❑ Rosé
❑ Sparkling ❑ Dessert ❑ Other

COLOR:

_____

AROMAS:

_____

DRY/SWEET: ❑ Bone-dry ❑ Dry ❑ Off-dry
❑ Medium-sweet ❑ Sweet

TANNINS: ❑ Low (easy to drink) ❑ Medium (balanced)
❑ High (bitter)

ACIDITY: ❑ Flat (very low) ❑ Soft (low)
❑ Balanced ❑ High (lively) ❑ Very high (bracing)

BODY: ❑ Light ❑ Medium ❑ Full

TEXTURE: ❑ Smooth ❑ Light ❑ Prickly/acidic
❑ Balanced ❑ Rough

TASTE:

FINISH: ❑ Short ❑ Medium ❑ Long

FOOD PAIRED WITH IT:

PAIRING SUCCESS: ❑ Disaster ❑ Okay, but not great
❑ Pretty good ❑ Fantastic

ADDITIONAL COMMENTS:

YOUR RATING:
☆　　☆☆　　☆☆☆　　☆☆☆☆　　☆☆☆☆☆

WINE:

PRODUCER:

| VINTAGE: | ALCOHOL %: | PRICE: |

REGION/COUNTRY:

GRAPE(S):

PLACE AND DATE PURCHASED:

| DATE TASTED: | IMPORTER/DISTRIBUTOR: |

COLOR/STYLE: ❑ Red ❑ White ❑ Rosé
❑ Sparkling ❑ Dessert ❑ Other

COLOR:

AROMAS:

DRY/SWEET: ❑ Bone-dry ❑ Dry ❑ Off-dry
❑ Medium-sweet ❑ Sweet

TANNINS: ❑ Low (easy to drink) ❑ Medium (balanced)
❑ High (bitter)

ACIDITY: ❑ Flat (very low) ❑ Soft (low)
❑ Balanced ❑ High (lively) ❑ Very high (bracing)

BODY: ❑ Light ❑ Medium ❑ Full

TEXTURE: ❑ Smooth ❑ Light ❑ Prickly/acidic
❑ Balanced ❑ Rough

TASTE:

_____

FINISH: ❑ Short ❑ Medium ❑ Long

FOOD PAIRED WITH IT:

_____

PAIRING SUCCESS: ❑ Disaster ❑ Okay, but not great
❑ Pretty good ❑ Fantastic

ADDITIONAL COMMENTS:

_____

_____

_____

YOUR RATING:
☆   ☆☆   ☆☆☆   ☆☆☆☆   ☆☆☆☆☆

WINE:

_____

PRODUCER:

_____

VINTAGE:	ALCOHOL %:	PRICE:

_____

REGION/COUNTRY:

_____

GRAPE(S):

_____

PLACE AND DATE PURCHASED:

_____

DATE TASTED:	IMPORTER/DISTRIBUTOR:

_____

COLOR/STYLE: ❑ Red   ❑ White   ❑ Rosé
❑ Sparkling   ❑ Dessert   ❑ Other

COLOR:

_____

AROMAS:

_____

DRY/SWEET: ❑ Bone-dry   ❑ Dry   ❑ Off-dry
❑ Medium-sweet   ❑ Sweet

TANNINS: ❑ Low (easy to drink)   ❑ Medium (balanced)
❑ High (bitter)

ACIDITY: ❑ Flat (very low)   ❑ Soft (low)
❑ Balanced   ❑ High (lively)   ❑ Very high (bracing)

BODY: ❑ Light   ❑ Medium   ❑ Full

TEXTURE: ❑ Smooth   ❑ Light   ❑ Prickly/acidic
❑ Balanced   ❑ Rough

TASTE:

_____

FINISH: ❑ Short   ❑ Medium   ❑ Long

FOOD PAIRED WITH IT:

_____

PAIRING SUCCESS: ❑ Disaster   ❑ Okay, but not great
❑ Pretty good   ❑ Fantastic

ADDITIONAL COMMENTS:

_____

_____

_____

YOUR RATING:
☆   ☆☆   ☆☆☆   ☆☆☆☆   ☆☆☆☆☆

WINE:

PRODUCER:

| VINTAGE: | ALCOHOL %: | PRICE: |

REGION/COUNTRY:

GRAPE(S):

PLACE AND DATE PURCHASED:

| DATE TASTED: | IMPORTER/DISTRIBUTOR: |

COLOR/STYLE: ❑ Red   ❑ White   ❑ Rosé
❑ Sparkling   ❑ Dessert   ❑ Other

COLOR:

AROMAS:

DRY/SWEET: ❑ Bone-dry   ❑ Dry   ❑ Off-dry
❑ Medium-sweet   ❑ Sweet

TANNINS: ❑ Low (easy to drink) ❑ Medium (balanced)
❑ High (bitter)

ACIDITY: ❑ Flat (very low) ❑ Soft (low)
❑ Balanced ❑ High (lively) ❑ Very high (bracing)

BODY: ❑ Light ❑ Medium ❑ Full

TEXTURE: ❑ Smooth ❑ Light ❑ Prickly/acidic
❑ Balanced ❑ Rough

TASTE:

_____

FINISH: ❑ Short ❑ Medium ❑ Long

FOOD PAIRED WITH IT:

_____

PAIRING SUCCESS: ❑ Disaster ❑ Okay, but not great
❑ Pretty good ❑ Fantastic

ADDITIONAL COMMENTS:

_____

_____

_____

YOUR RATING:
☆   ☆☆   ☆☆☆   ☆☆☆☆   ☆☆☆☆☆

WINE:

_____

PRODUCER:

_____

VINTAGE: | ALCOHOL %: | PRICE:

_____

REGION/COUNTRY:

_____

GRAPE(S):

_____

PLACE AND DATE PURCHASED:

_____

DATE TASTED: | IMPORTER/DISTRIBUTOR:

_____

COLOR/STYLE: ❑ Red   ❑ White   ❑ Rosé
❑ Sparkling   ❑ Dessert   ❑ Other

COLOR:

_____

AROMAS:

_____

DRY/SWEET: ❑ Bone-dry   ❑ Dry   ❑ Off-dry
❑ Medium-sweet   ❑ Sweet

TANNINS: ❏ Low (easy to drink)   ❏ Medium (balanced)
❏ High (bitter)

ACIDITY: ❏ Flat (very low)   ❏ Soft (low)
❏ Balanced   ❏ High (lively)   ❏ Very high (bracing)

BODY: ❏ Light   ❏ Medium   ❏ Full

TEXTURE: ❏ Smooth   ❏ Light   ❏ Prickly/acidic
❏ Balanced   ❏ Rough

TASTE:

_____

FINISH: ❏ Short   ❏ Medium   ❏ Long

FOOD PAIRED WITH IT:

_____

PAIRING SUCCESS: ❏ Disaster   ❏ Okay, but not great
❏ Pretty good   ❏ Fantastic

ADDITIONAL COMMENTS:

_____

_____

_____

YOUR RATING:
☆   ☆☆   ☆☆☆   ☆☆☆☆   ☆☆☆☆☆

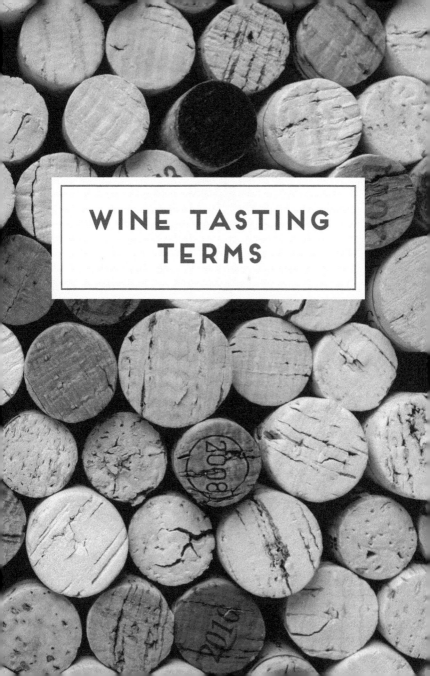

WINE TASTING
TERMS

Describing Flavors and Aromas

In this section you'll find a handy list of the most common terms for describing wine aromas and flavors, which you can use to quickly and efficiently find just the right tasting note for your journaling. They are grouped by type, from broader impressions (like tropical fruit) to specifics (e.g., pineapple).

The categories are in order of how most wines present their aromas and flavors, starting with primary (from the grape variety), then secondary (flavors developed through the winemaking process), and finally tertiary (developed through aging).

While this list is extensive, it's not exhaustive. Remember, what really counts is your personal impression, so use the terms that work best for you.

FRUIT

Berries

Blackberry

Black currant (cassis)

Black raspberry

Blueberry

Boysenberry

Cranberry

Gooseberry

Raspberry

Red currant

Strawberry

Citrus

Grapefruit

Lemon

Lime

Mandarin orange

Orange

Dried/Cooked Fruit

Apricot

Date

Fig

Marmalade/jammy

Prune

Raisin

Sultana/golden raisin

Tropical Fruit

Banana

Guava

Lychee

Mango

Passion fruit

Pineapple

Pomegranate

Starfruit

Other Fruit

Apricot (fresh)

Black cherry

Elderberry

Grape

Green apple

Honeydew melon

Nectarine

Peach

Pear

Plum

Quince

Red apple

Sour cherry

Yellow apple

VEGETAL/HERBACEOUS

Beet

Black olive

Canned peas

Cooked artichokes

Cooked asparagus

Cooked green beans

Cucumber

Cut grass

Dill

Eucalyptus

Green bell pepper

Green olive

Green tea

Hay/straw

Jalapeño

Laurel/bay leaf

Lemongrass

Lentil

Mint

Rhubarb

Rosemary

Sage

Tea leaf

Thyme

SPICE

Anise/licorice

Black pepper

Cinnamon

Cloves

Tomato

Tomato leaf

Ginger

Nutmeg

Vanilla

White pepper

FLORAL

Acacia

Bergamot (Earl Grey tea)

Cherry blossom

Elderflower

Geranium

Honeysuckle

Jasmine

Lavender

Lilac

Linden

Orange blossom

Peony

Rose

Violet

NUTTY

Almond

Coconut

Hazelnut

Peanut

Walnut

SWEET

Bubblegum	Fruitcake
Butterscotch	Honey
Buttery	Malt
Candy	Molasses
Caramel	Toffee
Chocolate/cocoa	White chocolate

MINERAL OR CHEMICAL

Diesel	Pencil shavings/graphite
Flint	Plastic
Granite	Slate
Kerosene	Sulfur (burnt match, rotten
Menthol	eggs, cooked cabbage,
Metallic	garlic, skunk, rubber)
Nail polish remover	Tar
Oxidized	Wet rocks

WOODY, SMOKY, OR TOASTED

Bacon	Oak
Cedar	Pine/resin
Cigar box	Sandalwood
Coffee	Smoked meat
Espresso	Toast
Leather	Tobacco

FERMENTED

Balsamic vinegar	Soy sauce
Bread	Sweaty
Brioche	Yeasty
Cheesy	Yogurt
Sauerkraut	

EARTHY OR BIOLOGICAL

Barnyard	Mushroom
Dried leaves	Musk
Horsey	Potting soil
Moldy/wet basement/wet cardboard	Truffle
	Wet dog
Mousy	Wet wool/lanolin

FAVORITE
BOTTLES

WINE: | **PAGE #:**

❑ Everyday ❑ Splurge

WINE: | **PAGE #:**

❑ Everyday ❑ Splurge

WINE: | **PAGE #:**

❑ Everyday ❑ Splurge

WINE: | **PAGE #:**

❑ Everyday ❑ Splurge

WINE: | **PAGE #:**

❑ Everyday ❑ Splurge

WINE: | **PAGE #:**

❑ Everyday ❑ Splurge

WINE: | **PAGE #:**

❑ Everyday ❑ Splurge

WINE: | **PAGE #:**

❑ Everyday ❑ Splurge

WINE: | **PAGE #:**

❑ Everyday ❑ Splurge

WINE: | **PAGE #:**

❑ Everyday ❑ Splurge

WINE: | **PAGE #:**

❑ Everyday ❑ Splurge

WINE: | **PAGE #:**

❑ Everyday ❑ Splurge

WINE: | **PAGE #:**

❑ Everyday   ❑ Splurge

WINE: | **PAGE #:**

❑ Everyday   ❑ Splurge

WINE: | **PAGE #:**

❑ Everyday   ❑ Splurge

WINE: | **PAGE #:**

❑ Everyday   ❑ Splurge

WINE: | **PAGE #:**

❑ Everyday   ❑ Splurge

WINE: | **PAGE #:**

❑ Everyday   ❑ Splurge

WINE: | **PAGE #:**

___

❑ Everyday   ❑ Splurge

WINE: | **PAGE #:**

___

❑ Everyday   ❑ Splurge

WINE: | **PAGE #:**

___

❑ Everyday   ❑ Splurge

WINE: | **PAGE #:**

___

❑ Everyday   ❑ Splurge

WINE: | **PAGE #:**

___

❑ Everyday   ❑ Splurge

WINE: | **PAGE #:**

___

❑ Everyday   ❑ Splurge

WINES
TO TRY

WINE:

PRODUCER:

WHO RECOMMENDED IT:

WINE:

PRODUCER:

WHO RECOMMENDED IT:

WINE:

PRODUCER:

WHO RECOMMENDED IT:

WINE:

PRODUCER:

WHO RECOMMENDED IT:

WINE:

_____

PRODUCER:

_____

WHO RECOMMENDED IT:

_____

WINE:

_____

PRODUCER:

_____

WHO RECOMMENDED IT:

_____

WINE:

_____

PRODUCER:

_____

WHO RECOMMENDED IT:

_____

WINE:

_____

PRODUCER:

_____

WHO RECOMMENDED IT:

_____

WINE:

_____

PRODUCER:

_____

WHO RECOMMENDED IT:

_____

WINE:

_____

PRODUCER:

_____

WHO RECOMMENDED IT:

_____

WINE:

_____

PRODUCER:

_____

WHO RECOMMENDED IT:

_____

WINE:

_____

PRODUCER:

_____

WHO RECOMMENDED IT:

_____

WINE:

_____

PRODUCER:

_____

WHO RECOMMENDED IT:

_____

WINE:

_____

PRODUCER:

_____

WHO RECOMMENDED IT:

_____

WINE:

_____

PRODUCER:

_____

WHO RECOMMENDED IT:

_____

WINE:

_____

PRODUCER:

_____

WHO RECOMMENDED IT:

_____

 **JOE ROBERTS** is a writer, blogger, video personality, wine critic, and frequent wine-competition judge whose work has appeared in publications as varied as Playboy.com and *Parade*. He's best known as the iconoclastic voice behind 1WineDude.com, one of the most awarded and influential wine blogs in the world. He is also the author of *Wine Taster's Guide: Drink and Learn with 30 Wine Tastings*. Roberts makes his living traveling the globe to discover off-the-beaten-path wine gems, as well as writing and talking about the world of wine and wine marketing. He lives near Philadelphia with his daughter, Lorelai. When his hands aren't in a notebook, at the keyboard, or holding a wine glass, he's playing bass guitar with the Steve Liberace Band.